T0123183

The Book of Jon

Dana S. Redman

authorHOUSE®

AuthorHouse™
1663 Liberty Drive
Bloomington, IN 47403
www.authorhouse.com
Phone: 1 (800) 839-8640

Published by AuthorHouse 12/22/2016

ISBN: 978-1-5246-5495-5 (sc)
ISBN: 978-1-5246-5494-8 (e)

Print information available on the last page.

Foreword

The Book of Jon, is a book of love, loss, life, and every day feelings and thoughts written on paper from my heart and mind. Through all of the ups and downs of life, no greater gift can give or receive, but Love.

Dana S Redman

ALL THE WHILE

All the time spent trying to fix it,
all the thunder,
all the rain,
all the hurt,
all the pain,
All the dried tears that left their stain.
Only the neglect in the end remain.

All the while in denial, pain and comfort devours the soul and in the end there is no one to hold.
The burden of loneliness is your constant friend for it will never leave you until the end.
When the last ember smoldering finally dies out, the burden is lifted and there's no more doubt.

All the while in a state of futile, destiny uncertain will be your final curtain.
The scars are there to remind you of all the years past hurting.
All the time you spent hard working, but it's still never enough, the edges of a heart can be jagged and rough like a cliffhanger the ascent can be tough.
You dig and claw to move up but in the end you crack like cheap glass of a cup.

All the while what you got anything good will die and rot. Even when it rains afterwards it again gets hot.
There's no real relief to have love, you have to steal it like a thief.

All the while all you want is a pure honest love of a friend to have to hold and understand. To love you every day over and over again, Loving you all the while.

Dana S Redman

Arrowhead In A Bottle

Earlier this year I received a gift of an arrowhead in a bottle from someone dear.
I destroyed what we had, what could have been went away with doubt and fear.
What I feel and felt in my heart was a solid sureness that we'd never grow apart.
Then doubt kept setting in from the depression and fear, of not being good enough one again. Do I deserve someone this good will I measure up like I should?

The first and only woman I completely trusted with all of me, never a doubt never a question.
She was all honest and true and talked to me and made me like myself like no one ever did or could do.
She went away never gave her a reason to stay,
I still have the arrowhead, the bottle shattered as it fell to the floor.
Like her feeling and trust hurt by man once more.
Do I love her, more than words can say,
I think of her every day?

She completed me she was the one,
we made each other laugh and made us feel finally we belonged to someone,
but I let everyone else control what I feel,
never followed my heart or too the time to heal.
I hurt her so badly like the broken bottle.
I thirst for her love but now will receive no drink or not even a swallow.

No one to blame but myself and my shame.
She deserved more than for her heart to be maimed,
I'm so sorry my friend,
I will always love you until my life comes to an end.

May there always be lilacs to smell along the way
and may you hear and feel I love you each and every day.
That's what I pray.

Dana S. Redman

Bethlehem Star

When I die, don't cry for me.
I'm going to heaven and now I'm free.
If you look to the heaven's sky at night look for a star that shines so bright.
That is me telling you I'm ok and if you need me, I will guide your way.
I didn't want to go, but no longer, I can stay.

I see a bright light and followed it, so know that I'm ok.
I had a great life, was so blessed to have my kids and my wonderful wife.
Look at those memories that we made, the hunting, fishing, and escapades.
The camping with family and all those trips, the hugs and the kisses from my family's lips.
I'm not hurting and now walk just fine.
I'm walking with Grandpa and Jesse they said hi and their fine.

I raised my children to look up to me, so look a little higher and you will see.
The star that shines brighter, hey!
That's me.

Dana S. Redman

Birds of Prey

Jon went away on that December day,
but I know in my heart he's flying high as a bird of prey.
I cried until I couldn't cry no more.
His death so close to my Dad's death before.
A slam to my heart, face and so much more.
Like the slam of tomb as you shut the door.
Jon loved hawks, eagles and falcons.
He's smile wide as he pointed one out.
So I know he's up there, there is no doubt.
I can't believe he's gone.
I feel like life has gone so wrong.

My Dad first, then Jon, makes it hard to smile, but I must live on.
Jon and Dad would want me to be strong.
So I will look to the sky and feel the heartache and at times cry.
Question God and ask him why.

I will see that eagle as he soars the wind, gliding high as he scans the scenery.
The osprey on the river diving for his dinner.
The kestrel hawk plucking the dove in my yard.
The red tail hawk hitting the rabbit in the meadow knocking it down hard.

Jon's there flying free without a care.
Watching over the ones still here.
Showing me, hey, I'm still near.
Don't cry for me, no more tears.
I'm free on the wind, I'm a bird of prey,

I had to go even though I wanted to stay.
So I'm halfway there and halfway here,
so don't you fear.

I loved you and loved you dear, so I won't go too far away you hear.
Listen to the red tail hawk in that meadow, it may be me and that's what I settled.
That heaven can wait and it's a hint to you I'm not or won't be seeing the devil.
I'm on a higher level and a bird of prey is my honor and medal.

Dana S Redman

Blankets of Loneliness

It's a blanket that's endless, the deficiency of love and acceptance.
The lack of acknowledgement and respect,
the wondering is this as good as it gets.
The hurt is horrendous,
the doubt is stupendous from the lack of the tenderness.
The world is so dark at times it seems,
you look for the light or even a gleam.

Dana S. Redman

BOOK OF JON

If I wrote a book, it would be a book of Jon,
from the first day I met him it was on.
Like a light switch, it was on.
our friendship a special bond.
So many memories the stories could go on and on.
No stronger love of brothers and with a warning or a sound.
It was lost as fast as it was found,
like a man that can't swim, Jon saved me and let me in.
He loves me like a brother even though we had different fathers and mothers.
We had dreams and fulfilled a few but looked forward to the adventures of new,
no man other than my Dad was true.

He was American as red, white and blue,
part Native American which made him even better,
a true woodsman of love and true spirit forever.
He brought me luck and I to him.
We always did well together, apart it was sink and each other swim.
Jon was a very hard book to read, a private man yes indeed,
a hard life made him,
and pride of his past made walls that few were let in.
He softened as the years went by, our parents passed and I see him cry.
So much heartache, so many died, and then he went away and watches me cry.
I look at his pictures every day, but I feel him close in every way.
Why did he go and I had to stay, God I guess planned it that way.
His thunderous voice and spontaneous laugh, oh the stories of the past.

The book of Jon is here at last, from the first shot to the last cast,
Jon was my future, present and past.
A lifelong friend like no other, he was my friend but more my brother.
I lost my twin and seven days later my mom went right back into labor.
Delivered a sack of an unborn twin, well here's where it's cool a twin born again.
You see my birthday is March 21st, Jon's was March 28th, same year.

So here is the book of Jon, I lost my twin and God gave me him,
so both of us could live on.
He saved me and I saved him, we opened our hearts and let the other in.

Dana S. Redman

Brother

What is a brother,
is a brother born of the same father and mother,
well yes, indeed, the same seed.

What makes a brother, the same blood or love shown,
the friendship and bond of a friend always known.
To call a man brother is respect given and shown
and the years shared and the friendship grown.

I lost a friend that was a brother to me all my life I'd known,
Now my brother is gone,
the three times a week conversations, the laughter, love and life's frustrations.
The years came and went,
we would talk for hours about hunting or sometimes to cry and vent.

What makes a brother,
in God's eyes, we all are sister and brothers,
in his image from centuries of fathers and mothers.
I was blessed with a dear, dear friend, a brother to me until his end. A bond that could never be broken or bend.
Solid as a firm handshake, a nod, a smile, a mend.
We did all that we loved to do,
at times I was the pupil, other times I was the teacher,
and at times just a lost fool.

The memories we made, the laughter we shared,
The emotions laid down when our hearts were bared.
The fly fishing, elk hunts, the stories of bucks.
When we were together it always was good luck.
We complimented each other in so many ways.
Never thought that I'd lose my brother so soon on that December day.
Never thought that he'd go away.
If I could just tell him one time and say,
I will always love you my brother,
and miss you every day.

Dana S Redman

Center Punch

You took out your anvil and punch,
stuck it to my chest and drove it in on a hunch.
No little starter prick, oh no, that's not your style.
A full thrust pounding and where I stood at my feet there laid a pile.
The walls that you hammered, the rubble that fell.
I wonder still what you see in me but anymore you hardly tell.
I missed so much before I met you,
you showed me my worth in the few words that you tell.

You've had me since center punch,
you drove your love into me like a wrecking machine,
so much that I couldn't handle the force and the speed.
In the end result, it's you that I need.

I close my eyes and see your face,
I dream of you my heart is at a race.
I wake to your call or just a hello and at times my legs feel just like Jell-O.

I hope you feel my love from me too,
so you'll know truly how much I love you.
Let me walk through a storm for you,
you're the fire that gives me warmth,
you're the reason I'm still here.

Center punch so long ago and still losing you is my fear.
I love you forever or always,
center punched and crystal clear.

Dana S Redman

Chutes and Ladders

Chutes and Ladders is a game,
life is no different and so much the same.
You climb high and struggle for so long,
you keep climbing and you feel your confident get strong.
You put people up there along with you to make them feel they belong too.
You keep climbing as high as you can stand,
or at least to the people that want or demand.
One wrong step, one slip and you fall.
All that you strived for is gone,
for you lose it all.

The higher you climb, the farther you slide,
momentum will take you all the way down,
and in the end you are alone with no one by your side.

Chutes and Ladders is life at times,
your heart shattered and left with a scattered mind.
It is not the slide that gets you,
it is the sudden stop, the pain and injury and the distance from the top.
You worked so hard to get ahead, but in the end you are alone instead.
Only God is really by your side, for he sacrificed his Son, blood and died.

Chutes and Ladders is a game, but in life you are hurt from the pain.
You laugh, you cry, you strive for good,
but in the end, you're alone and feel that there was more to do if you could.
You are born to three and you end with one,
and so quick in life everything can come undone.

Chutes and Ladders, Love and hate,
give all you can,
and some all they do is just want more to take, so slide down from where you once elevate.

Chutes and Ladders,
love is the only thing that matters,
but in your soul you are sadder and left heart shattered.
Was the climb worth the effort when love is lost and the fall leaves you tattered.
Fear of heights in the end, scared to climb, and hurt again,
scared to slide down the chute and be lost and alone,
to fall too hard and hit like a stone,
in the end break every bone.

Dana S. Redman

E Pluribus Unum

I don't want to be just somebody because of comparison of everybody,
I don't want to be a great guy to be compared to a nobody.
I'm not an E Pluribus Unum.

No comparison of the past, but an equal determined.
I don't want to be a somebody, not one of some,
Not an E Pluribus Unum.

I want the union,
just me to not be compared while my heart is wide open left exposed and barred.
Be good enough for them that the love will last,
not be better looking or a harder worker than the ones of the past.

The older I get the more I'm compared to the ones of before that failed or didn't pass,
what the woman really needed, so it would have been her only and last.

I am just me, never seen nothing great,
I lived all my life as a giver and no take,
I wear my heart on my sleeve exposed to all things.
Leaving it there for some to take,
not to abuse or use up what's left.
To hold it close to theirs, tight to their breast
and maybe realize in no comparison of the past that they have found the best,
on their own plateau of love way above all the rest.

Dana S. Redman

Everything Ends with A "D" at the End

You go through life all you want to be is loved,
but life has its struggles and ups and downs, smiles and frowns.
You as a child want to be loved and accepted,
time goes on as a teenager you feel defective.
You get married and you think you found the one, but it's a big letdown.
You feel defeated, disheartened, distraught and depleted.
Your heart is shattered like you never mattered,
the tears leave a story from the dry splatter.
You put all you can into that life, you wanted to be that man to the greatest wife.
The love that was there was cut away like a knife.
You feel like your nothing because that's what you have felt so long.
Everything ends with a 'D' at the end.
You want your spouse to be your best friend.
You feel like a big disappointment.
You got married for a lifelong anointment.

They treat you wonderful in the beginning,
hoping the life will be what you're dreaming.
In the ending it's a divorce,
they took all you had but not by force.
You cry so many times wanting that reach or acknowledgment so you'll be fine.
It doesn't happen, the dark gets darker, the struggle so much harder.

Your life is shorter and all out of disorder,
everything ends with a 'D' at the end all you want is a lifelong friend.
All you want is a five letter word for your life in the end, loved.
Before death is the mend.

Dana S. Redman

Fire for Effect

You always fire for effect,
what does it do, for there is no benefit?
Everything great you tore down and destroyed.
All that you left me was a deep, empty void.
All the greatness you were, you destroyed with your words.
You shattered my hope and stomped on my care.
You shot and crippled me like a wounded game bird.

No dog will find me for that is not in the cards,
but you fire for effect to hurt me, and me stop loving who you are.
Every word hurtful took more of the good away,
one word after another until you shot down all I could say.

Fire for effect,
don't know how much you killed until the smoke clears and the hurt you can finally hear.
The moans and the cries, the cease fires and the love dies.
No time for a white flag, just angry goodbyes.
You took all the good and stomped it out like a fire.

When the embers die out, the relationship is dead.
Nothing I say to you is the truth, for all is a lie to you, so nothing can be said.
It is a tragic destruction of what once was so good,
so you fired for effect until no longer I stood.
Then questioned the reason why I can stand for no more.
As everything solid is shot to hell and feeling poor,

you shot out in anger until nothing was left,
you standing with a smoking gun until you seen my last breath.
You sit there and wonder why your life is such a disarray,
for anger and failure is what you expect every day.

So failure you embrace and loss is what you hold,
and anything new you are in a hurry to make old.
So keep on shooting,
don't aim, just spray,
anything left living will just walk away.

Dana S. Redman

Holding onto Nothing

You hold on to nothing, until that's the way you feel about yourself.
Can't find any more of your self-wealth.
You keep plugging along, trying to be strong.
All you want is to be loved all along, so you keep holding on to nothing,
every day is the same without the loving.
So you work harder for your escape,
you keep giving and never take.

For if you do you feel less in you,
so you keep giving to try to make the love renew.
Holding onto nothing all you want is the touching and loving.
When you try to give yours away it's more like a smothering,
so you get pushed away from your touch or what you say,
you live it through day by day.
You grab onto any good word they say,
so you can get through some way.

You beg, plead and even pray,
it bounces back to you to stay.
In the end you feel like your nothing,
because you held on to it so long,
anything else would be something.

Dana S. Redman

I Am Not Much

I am not much, but I am me.
I cannot beg if you cannot see. I need you, you need me.
Please do tell me to let you be, I will give you time,
if you give yourself to me.
I hope someday your past will set you free, see all that I can see.

Heal some of your misery,
make the years past history.
Sometimes I cry all night long for I want so much to belong,
wonder why I have been wronged,
feeling lost like a forgotten song.
I have nothing but me to give,
I could be one reason God wanted you to live.
And I can show you I am the real deal.
Give me time and time to heal,
Maybe I love you enough that you will heal.
I am not a thief that is going to steal,
I am not much; I am just me.
Take the blinders off and you will see,
you already see so much in me.

I hope someday where I am at you may want to be,
I will wait and see.
I am so scared of growing old,
My love is not the marked to be bought and sold.
The loneliness it seems so cold,
If I was a loner hand, I would fold.

I am not great man to me,
so I do not expect you to see me be.

I am just me, living every day in the dark hoping for the sun to see. I am not rich, I am not poor,
I live on no marble or dirt floor.
I am in between for it was what I worked for.
I am just me, which I am not much.
Been overlooked and forgotten from my words to my touch,
I am just me,
So you see just hope I am good enough for you.

Dana S. Redman

I Never

I never thought it would turn out like this.
Never forget your sweet kiss.
Never will stop loving you,
but can't fix me and can't fix you.
So much happiness you gave to me.
Then I fell apart and ask you to let me be.
I'm not free, but in your eyes that's what you see.
I never thought I would hurt you,
fall in love and then desert you.
So much has happened between you and I,
just life has happened, the loss and the why.
So many loved ones said goodbye, I question God and ask why.
Seen you today, just drive by, inside my heart and soul I cry.
Your negativity drove me away,
but in my heart you'll always stay.
I will always love you no matter what you believe or say,
I'm not ready for you, I thought I was, but instead I hurt you.
I couldn't handle how you were,
but I thought I could change you and make you happy girl.
This is my loss, my bad timing, my cost.
I'm so very sorry that what we had is gone,
I thought and felt that we belonged, how much I was wrong.
I never will forget our songs,
just can't forget all the wrongs.

Dana S. Redman

I Will Always Look Up

You planted the seeds and helped us grow,
all I am and what I know is what you taught me in the show.
You never said I love you much but showed it every day so we would know. I knew this day would someday come, but it is too hard to let you go.
You were and always will be my best friend,
Whenever I felt broken, you were the mend.
Everything good about me came from you again and again for my last name is Redman.
I have looked up to you all my life,
always appreciated how much love you showed my children and wife.
I remember all the good times and some of the bad,
but all in all I remember how awesome a man you were and are,
and how bless I was to call you Dad.
I remember how you always strived to work hard with all your pride.
How you were always honest and never lied, how you would get so mad if you lost at cards,
and how you taught Steve, Suzanne, and I to work so hard.

You taught us to hunt, trap, and fish,
I wish I could go back to those days again, once as a kid, a week or two would be my wish,
so many memories have given to me,
all the times in the woods whether it was hunting, trapping, fishing, cutting wood, or identifying trees.
Work always came and I was not always happy when you asked or ordered.

But that time we shared made me who I am and compared to you I feel, at times I fall short in that order.

To be with you anytime gave me pride and joy and peace of mind.
I love you Dad for a Dad like you is hard to find.
A man like you, after all you have been through, makes you truly one of a kind.
I wish I could have passed on all you showed to me, but it is so hard in this electronic society.
Makes it hard to show them all the things we know and did.
I knew this day was coming, but I believe God intervened,
for now the pain is numbing, or so it seems.
I wish I was half the man that you were always to me.
For in my heart and mind you were my hero of all time.

I love you always, have been so bless to call you Dad.
It is hard to let go of someone so great. Don't know how long my heart will ache.
So go see Great Grandpa, Grandma Henry, Ed Doering, Uncle Ben, my twin, and Grandpa too,
tell them I miss the, but most of all,
I'll be missing you.

Dana S. Redman

If I Could Take It

If I could take it, I would and maybe do it for the better good. Take you pain if I could.
Love you more when no one would.
If I could take your hurt and make it go away,
take your place and die if you could stay.
If I could take the hurt absorb it like a sponge,
so you could always smile and laugh living life and having fun.

If I could take it, take your place,
never see again the pain come across your face.
If I could reach into your soul,
pull out all the heartache and the past tears that have rolled,
Then I would and never hesitate to make you happy,
so that you have no more heartache.
If I could take it I would hold your head in my hands,
look you in the eyes so you know I understand.
Kiss the tears away from that moment on and every single day,
make you happy in every way.

If I could take it and your place, I would go for you to stay.
So you would know I love you in every way,
for I cannot stand or handle you ever going away.
I would let God take me instead if I could have my way.
As long as you keep living,
I would gladly take your place as you watch me go away.

Dana S. Redman

If You

If you let me in will you let me stay?
Will you take my hand and lead the way?
Will you kneel down with me and daily pray.
Will you leave me and walk away?
If you let me in, will you let me stay, will you take in all I have to say, will you love me through the years each and every day.
If you let me in, will you close the door so only I can love you forever more.
Whether we are rich or dirt, floor poor, will I always be what you were looking for.

Will I be the one you've always adored,
If you open up and let me in, if I grow tired and no longer swim, even if you can't, will you jump in and save me again.
Will you always be first my friend and be that way with me until my life ends.
If you let in will you let me stay, will you take my hand and show the way.
Will you love me each and every day,
And will you let me in completely and allow me to love you along the way.

Dana S. Redman

I'M A TREE

I've stood through tragedies and storms,
remained standing and somewhat damaged form.
I've seen snow, I've seen rain, ice and sunshine, and I remain.
I've seen darkness and days of beauty.
Autumn splendors like a guard on duty.
I've been beaten by hail and wind, scratched on by brothers and hit with bigger limbs.
I'm a tree,
I continue to stand not as handsome as years have left their brand.

I'm a tree,
I have roots well bedded in this ground.
My seeds from my father and forefathers that been handed on down.
I have seeds here too, they blew in the wind, I don't see them like I used too.
I know they're around, but that's all I know,
I don't see them often but can sense them when the wind blows.
They are my future and I am their past,
but I will live in them and the seeds that they make, so I will last.
Generation upon generation stood to the storm.
We are a well-rooted family of strong willed and solid form.
We will try hard to stand our ground and belong.

I'm a tree,
the years have showed, the scars, and broken structure.
All the wounds that didn't heal all the visual punctures.
The inside of my body is hollow somewhat,

but I'm not dead yet so don't cut me down where I stand.
I'm still alive and want to live for as long as I can.
Just because I'm damaged doesn't mean I'm completely useless my friend.
I've gave life to others, comfort to the cold,
coolness and kindness when the sun seemed so bold.
I've gave your ears kind gestures, put smiles on your face.
Gave you direction with the moss on my north face.
In the fall I've given you a golden landscape and I still remain.
I've lost so much in this life and concurred so much pain.
I still stand tall after all these long years,
if you could make leaves into teardrops then you could imagine the tears.
I stand here so lonely and miss so much interaction,
someday I may go down,
but only by God's satisfaction.

For I have a purpose here more than just planting seeds,
to be respected and looked upon and be trusted and at ease.
For I have never faltered to wind or no storm,
I've fought all my life to survive since a seedling I was born.

I am a tree,
and strong I remain,
acknowledgement is what I seek,
only lightning can take me down and lack of love is my pain,
but here I am and stand,
I remain.

Dana S. Redman

Last Man Standing

It's not easy being the left behind.
Life is short as God designed.
Death is slow, or fast without a warning or a sign,
and your left last man standing and left behind.
The tears fall, your heartaches a constant reminder of how life is so precious until the break.
Last man standing, in the dark, with a calloused heart.
Want them back, but they won't come, only the memories will on.
Last man standing, shed the most tears, from all the loss over the living years.
The heartache goes from death to death, who will die next is just a guess.
You drudge on and live for them, so many loved ones, so many friends.
Hoping someday you'll reunite with your loved ones again.
You see life and you feel death, and only God knows your final breath.
I love him for he made me and with his love then death wouldn't be such a misery.
Hopefully heaven is my final destiny, and because of his love I feel empathy.
Last man standing, is the last man that cries,
last man standing is the one with the most goodbyes.
I miss so many, did God miss me,
only time will tell when the end is near that's life's mystery and the living fear.
So love everybody that are dear.
You may live long or death is near.

If you love the Lord, then there is no fear.
The last man standing shed the most tears.
The last man standing is the one who cried the most,
the last one to meet him and the last one to become a ghost.

Dana S Redman

LIKE A BOOK

If you would open me like a book, read all of me and take a deeper look.
Don't skip through the pages but read me word for word.
Take them to your heart so your mind can have them heard.
Don't break the binding and bend me too far,
for that holds my spine and I don't want to lose my heart.

So read me like a book,
each paragraph and chapter so you know the story and know I was worth a second look.
Read between the lines of why I am me and what God designed.
I'm no novel but I'm not a paperback that can be thrown away in a garbage sack.
I'm as real as real can be, you won't find me in fiction or the section of comedy.
I'm a damn biography, how I end up maybe a mystery.
I would like a love story, but that's up to you.
The fear is I might find you in history.

So read me like a book, since you took the time to look,
I hope I leave you hanging word for word,
let your heart feel and mind register each and every word.
Let me be read silent or aloud, so each and every word be heard.

Read me like a book and never put me away,
hold it to your chest
and silently say to yourself,
I read the best.

Dana S Redman

Like a River

She's like a river so strong,
her beauty and soul go on and on.
She cuts deep and she cuts fast,
her love runs through you and is so vast,
it's a love that always will last.

From her beginning to her end,
she'll flow deeply through the rapids and every bend.
There is no pretend,
her current is fast and furious when she is mad,
and at times the water reseeds when she is happy and glad.
Her pools are deep full of care so happy to have you so blessed that you're there.

She's like river that runs so deep,
her brown eyes lose you and you would drown,
she doesn't have to say a word but the words you can read in her eyes are profound.

She's like a river ever flowing, so independent and always going.
Her love like the water, flows everywhere,
if only I could stay in it, then I'd always feel her care.

I know where she flows and at times how she grows,
strong and majestic, destructive when she doesn't give a shit.
She's peaceful and calm when the time is right but if things don't set well she's an unstoppable sight.
For she's like river so beautiful and serene,

but if she comes over her banks and go out of her plane the destruction can be harmful to anyone downstream,
but oh, how I love her and to drown in her bliss,
to constantly be covered by her love and by her kiss.

Dana S. Redman

Live for Me

Jon has passed and my heart aches.
The emptiness of what God takes.
Jon was good and always will be,
and I know he's gone but if he could speak.
Live for me.

Shoot every grouse you see,
Live for me.

Love my kids, show them the way,
get down on your knees and pray,
Live for me.

Live on, stay strong,
don't cry that I'm gone.
Live for me.

Do all we said that we would do,
follow it through,
Live for me.

I am here, and not too far,
I'm the air you breathe,
I'm not in the stars you see,
I love you and you loved me and you still do I can see.
Live for me.

Shoot every long beard that you see,
shoot double, one for you and one for me,
Live for me.

Be all more than you can be, I'm right here by your side.
I believed in you that's why you cry.
I love you and you love me, spread my ashes where I want to be.
Live for me.

I didn't want to go,
I wanted to see my children grow.
Live for me.

Please brother,
live for me.

Shoot every big buck that you see,
shoot the other just for me,
Live for me.

Trap all the mink, raccoon too,
catch every trout like we use to.
Live for me, live long for me.

I miss you so,
I didn't really want to go,
Live for me.

Go to Alaska and shoot that moose,
go get that Elk, may your luck reverse,
I'll be there like I use to be,
look for that eagle that is me.
Live for me.
for I lived for you.

We weren't just friends, but brothers, through and through,
I believed in you, I still do,
so live for me Dana,
for I would live for you.

Dana S. Redman

Love Unaccepted

I feel like my love is undetected,
not good enough to be accepted.
How can the past make a heart so unreceptive?
How can pain make a hole,
where never again can be filled with love and let it flow.

Love unaccepted,
the hurt of the past makes you feel defective.
Even if you know the love is there,
you let them go for the care is there,
for you can't accept the love and do you dare.

I felt it oh so deep,
but the mountain of hurt was just way too steep.
I can break at any moment and begin to weep.
You think of them constantly,
your heart feels the love,
but the pain outweighs it constantly.
You tell them you need time to heal,
what they don't know is your lost and don't know how to heal.
The pain is constant and so surreal,
so you hurt the one that had love that's real.

Love unaccepted,
they take it to a personal perspective,
they blame themselves and you,
doubt the soul and end up blue.

You pray for forgiveness and for God to fix you,
broken and battered and torn in two.

You in time turned into something you're not,
wishing you would bleed and without a clot,
everything good you can't accept for you look in the mirror and all you see is a defect.
You want to be that person that you felt good about,
since the time you changed and fell apart.
You don't know that person you were,
and don't know the person you've become,
but the pain is what you feel and anything good is numb.
The love is buried deep within,
begging for forgiveness of your failures and sin.

Heartache and loss,
you just can't win.
Love in unaccepted is what did it in.

Dana S. Redman

Measuring Up

I'm not a cup full of sugar or a bucket of crap,
I'm in between as a matter of fact.
I want to matter and be matter,
I don't walk up hill all my life I went to take the path that flatter.
You opened me up and I shut all doors,
too scared to not be good enough and flat broke poor.

I am scared of measuring up,
sometimes when it's too good to be true it makes you give up.

When the reflection seems uninterested,
you think you're failing what you've been tested.
I know it's better to try and fail then not to try at all,
but when your whole life has been subjected to failure you're scared looking through your walls.

All I can see is yours through the view,
scared of what I feel and of what you'll do, to me and you.
So I worried if I measured up too scared to fail and not make the cut.
Cared too much about your feeling too,
now I've put you back out there and you're going out to show and prove.
I feel somehow I've already lost you.
When someone finds that person that fits, it's a shock to the system in spite of it.

When you look into someone else's soul and that really where you want to inhabit,
then you also find yourself caring more for their soul then your own and as fast as it came,
it will be gone.

I've not always measured up,
but if you were the fountain of love then let me forever sip from your cup,
but only if I measure up.

Dana S. Redman

Memory Maker

You were always a memory maker,
always a giver never much of a taker.
All you gave in not enough thanks.
You were my scholar my mentor, my professor and friend.
You taught me so much, right up to the end.
Whatever was broken you had a mend.
You were my teacher, my hero, my friend.

Whenever I was lost,
it was you I seek for guidance in, again and again.
You taught me to be a man and oh how I've tried,
you taught me to be honest and never to lie.
The hardest thing in my life I knew was to every have you die.
For you're too great to me to ever say goodbye.

You were always a memory maker,
you were the glue that kept us together, like dough to a baker.
Always a hard worker never a task shaker.
Do it with pride until your last breath is gone with God the soul taker.
You were all my good memories maker.

I love you my Daddy, say hi to the maker.

Dana S Redman

Muddied Water

The water was crystal clear before I came along,
if only I would have stayed clear and left you where you belonged.
Instead I walked downstream to you,
muddied the water between me and you.
It was crystal clear so you could see right through,
but I muddied the water and your understanding,
so you couldn't even see where you were standing.
I should of damned it up, upstream from you,
then I never would of sent you debris
and you would have never even noticed me or that I was there, never made you love me or you showing me you care.

I muddied up the water like a tributary in the spring.
Churned up all that was clear and manageable.
Now the water is over the banks,
you walked away after you opened the flood gates.

Dana S. Redman

SAVING GRACE

She always has had saving grace,
an angel on earth with a different loving heart and a gracious face.
A crooked smile and genuine care,
someone honest, loyal and fair.
A woman so complex that she's so hard to read,
so wonderful with kindness, she's all that I need.
When she's sick or she's mad, then doubt may come in,
she's a completely different person then when she doesn't carry her grin.
She's complicated at best,
but she's nothing like the rest.
No manipulation, she is what she is,
no bullshit in her from her toes to her head.
She's saving grace, and I set that all back,
I lost what I had and now oh God how I lack.
I severed the trust the honesty and care,
wrecked twice the commitment and honesty there.

Turned into someone I've always despised turned into a liar,
but it both of us crying these tears that don't dry.
My biggest fear is a final goodbye.
I never deserved her, she's better than I.
She really loved me,
but I didn't believe, now she's gone forever, a distant melody.
I betrayed her so bad, broke her heart, made her sad.
Didn't feel good enough to accept what I had.

Now saving grace is all gone, I'll never belong.
She'll never trust what I wronged.
I let everyone manipulate me, worried about what everyone else thought or wanted,
but her and I are the ones broken hearted,
she's the one that feels not good enough and discarded.

I let my mind effect my heart let my doubt wash it out.
Her feelings were surreal, but my doubt ebbed the feel.
Insecurities made it unacceptable that saving grace was the real deal.
I love her still but I broke her trust, and her love that was real.
Will see love me still,
or what was there did I kill.

Dana S. Redman

Severing

It's all in the severance, the separation and isolation.
That your life in the stars is no constellation.
You're a shooting star a falling creation of Gods expectation.
You've become segregated from all you've known,
you're born of flesh and in the end become bone.
Born from death to become a living being to end up alone,
it's severing to the soul a place that no one will or wouldn't ever go.
Even when you open up the door,
no one looked inside, they'd just walk right by the corridor.
Separation of body and mind, hiding the frustration of what God designed,
severing trust, drive, and anything to live for.

To give all you've ever had and trying to give more.
In the end you're knocked to the floor,
to dust yourself off and see the other is keeping score.
Not enough of one thing or another, to broke and poor to be discovered.
Better to leave your heart buried and uncovered.
Separation of God and state, separation of love and hate, separation from happiness to break.
How much can one person take, it's all in the severing,
severe the lines that hold you strong,
cut the ties and your loss and you will not ever again belong.
Every right becomes so wrong, God suffered so much for me to belong,
why couldn't I be that strong,
love can save you or just string you along and in the end you'll never belong.

Dana S. Redman

SHALLOW GRAVE

Lay me in a shallow grave or put me in a darkened cave,
for love is all I crave.
Like a binder of a book,
I'm weakened with every touch and look.
No one will ever take the time to read between the lines,
they forget about all I've gave just complain on what I've took.

Bury me in a shallow grave so what the worms don't eat the predators can save.
That way I'm giving to more than one for everything I've gave have come undone.

Sick of being number two,
wish someday I could be number one.
I sleep on a stain filled pillow.
If I were a tree I'd be a weeping willow,
Weak to the weather and elements for my structure is weak and make up irrelevant.
At one time I was an oak,
strong and solid, and no matter what I could support the family and have doubt.
I would bend but never break,
my roots run deep from all the pounding in the world I could take.
Then time goes by for it really never is on your side,
and your center begins to weaken and rot.

You've given all you got and what you felt before is a mistake from the spot,
so bury me in a shallow grave,
love was all I ever wanted,
respect and appreciation is what I crave.

What I realize is in my life women don't want a good man,
they just want a man with all the goods.
Good guys finish last,
so throw me in quicksand or a lake so I'll got fast,
wash or rot away my past.
There are no guarantees, for nothing good lasts.

So bury me in a shallow grave,
dig me up if I'm worth the save or just re-dig a deeper grave.

Dana S. Redman

SHALLOWS

I'm here in the shallows,
scared to go deep,
scared to drown with no heart to beat.
I'm here in the shallows,
the water looks deep,
too scared to dive in and drown as I weep.
Too scared to fail,
Too scared to swim,
so I will remain in the shallows so I can breathe once again.

The water looks deep,
no narrow channel to swim.
It's all wide open right there in front of me again.
What if I get there only to be pushed back,
the water is calm now but what if I lack.
It could be choppy, waves could come in,
I'm not a strong swimmer and what if they won't want me again.
I'll be stuck in the deep too far to swim back,
too far from the shallows to avoid failure or lack.

I'm here in the shallows that's where I may remain.
To avoid any bad weather and to avoid all the pain.
Yes, I am lonely, but too scared to move on.
The land is behind me but so are the frowns.
I don't want to fail again but I do want to love,
only God can save me, but at times He is too far above.

I'm here in the shallows, the deep is right there,
but what if they quit seeing me or stop knowing I'm there.
I'm a cast away, forgotten for so long.
Even though I'm wanted, I don't feel good enough to belong.
Am I worthy enough to make my love stay strong,
or will I perish and sing to the bottom of the sea.
Like a ship going down, will they even search for me.

Dana S. Redman

SHELTER IN ME

No matter if I'm here or there, don't forget I'll always care.
When life is rough and you're feeling weak and not so tough.
You can find shelter in me.
When you're cold and your soul feels bought and then sold.
You can find shelter in me, just close your eyes and then you can see.
Feel the warmth of a friend who will care and love you,
Till the end no expectations or I.O.U's, just honesty and being true to pick you up when you're blue.
To put love in your heart and make it renewed.

When you're cold I'll warm you, never cheat you or disown you.
I'll sharpen your edges and hone you.
Make you sharp as a razor and in return expect no favor.
Give you hope in life and show you to enjoy every minute and each memory to savor.

Shelter in me,
so you have a place to always be a safe haven in me.
When you're hot and need some shade,
I'll cool you off like a glass of cold lemonade.
Show you God is proud of you and cares for you too,
and you'll know he's begotten and made.

I will give you all the shelter I can,
life you up when you need a hand,
shelter you to the wind when you cannot stand and always be your loving friend.

Dana S. Redman

SHIVER

If you were a star, you would be a shimmer.
If I was drowning you would be a strong swimmer.
I feel at times like I live with doubt, a loser at times, but you make me feel like a winner.
You give me that shiver that makes a man quiver like a deer shot in the liver.
He knows he is going to die, but he has to run or life will pass him by.
So he runs from the impact of the shot until he lays there and his last breath is taken,
and his last action is a shiver.

You are a shiver of hope, feelings you share and kind words spoke.
There is no pretend,
no falseness or misguiding,
just you and I finding each other while we are both surviving.
Shiver,
shiver of hope, glimmer of faith, glimpse of new,
so many great glimpses I see in you, so I shiver.
Shiver from the cold, when you are not there, shiver from the thought do I try to dare.
For I already gave and share, you already see I do care.

Hope, trust, and honesty I see in you and I know you see it too,
So you shiver from the thought, let him go or keep what you caught.
Walk away to avoid maybe feeling distraught,
What we see in each other cannot be borrow or brought.
So we shiver taking baby steps to avoid the fear of getting too near,

even though we enjoy the other and see very clear.
So you feel the spine tingling shiver, from the hopefulness of good we see in one another.
You see a good man and father, I see a beautiful, wonderful woman and mother.
We see so much of that that we are scared of one another. Unfortunately, we know there may be no other,
so we shiver.

Dana S. Redman

Standing Alone

I drove by an old homestead one day in the spring of this year
when everything is still dead and dormant from the winters cold and gray.
I looked out and in front of the old home,
there by itself it stood all alone,
a beautiful flower in the desolate place,
reminded me of you and your warm face.
Standing alone and sticking out in this world.
A wonderful creation, a blessing, a girl.
Standing alone in this dark, dreary race,
standing tough but beautiful, like so out of place.

You weathered the storms, the tragedy and the loss,
sometimes I'm sure it feels at all cost.
Standing alone like that flower that day, hoping someone will notice as they pass and stop to say, that you are so beautiful to stand where you stood,
all that you have strived for all that is good.
Hoping to be noticed, acknowledged and received,
scared they will leave like the autumn fall leaves.
Not to stay and weather the storm with you or just blow away.
So there you stand with the background of gray,
scenery of death.

Hoping they will see you and stop to smell you and feel their breath.
To acknowledge you is a blessing, but most just pass through.
Hope you know that I truly do love you.

I have noticed you always and always will do,
but at this time in my life, passing by is all I can do.
So from the distance I know who truly you are,
but unfortunately for both of us, I will just love you from afar.
A beautiful daffodil,
is just what you are.

Dana S. Redman

Taking Its Toll

Life is hard yes indeed,
every day is a gift from God, so blessed by every breath I breathe. I see the sun rise and it goes away.
Just like my loved ones, but I'm stuck and have to stay.
The older I get the more loss I see,
the more tears fall, the more heartache and misery.
It's taking its toll, each blow after another,
sometimes so close I just feel smothered.
I look up to God and ask him why,
so many loved ones that said goodbye.

So many sorrows, so many tears,
the longer I live through these losing years,
It's taking its toll, I feel the strain,
the tears that I shed have fell like rain.
The lost ones are here and always remaining.
They're here in my heart and always a thought in my brain.
The only evidence to the outside world is if they look closely they'll see a tear stain.
It's taking its toll but I shouldn't complain,
but I'm left here with nothing and alone I remain.
My comfort is in that they're in a better place and my companion is my pain.

Dana S Redman

Tear Bed

So many tears I've shed for you.
The trials and struggles you put me through.
The commitment is there,
but the trials seem to interfere.
I love you dear, I always have, hard to love until I'm sad,
So there's a tear bed.

A constant bed where you always flow,
a dry residue that you'll never lose your hold.
You carry my heart under your chest,
protect it with love, and show me your best.
Every day I want to wake to you,
holding me like you always do.
The away time is killing me,
only my pillow knows the tears that have been freed.
You complete me all the time, heart, soul, body and mind.
Love me, dry the tears, wash the tear bed away.
For I'm only a minute from losing you again, minute after minute, day after day.
I miss your smile, your goofy laugh, I love working with you and you being around.
You're my look forward when I'm feeling down.

I found a dry creek bed where once it flowed,
but not even a trickle or mud would show.
So mother nature took it away,
for a drought set in and a drought thus stay.

Until the weather rains more than enough,
the creek will stay dried up and look barren and tough.

So don't stop crying if you're missing me.
For I miss you terribly, just you don't get to see.
So a tear bed is here from my eye to my chin.
Oh, how I've loved you again and again.

You're not just a woman, but my dear, best friend.
I will always miss you and love you until the tears dry up or my life ends.

Dana S. Redman

THE BEAUTY WITHIN

The beauty within,
if we all would only search for the beauty within,
the world be a better place,
There would be more smiles and grins.
Nobody would feel the bitter loneliness or the coldness setting in,
the sadness sinking in.

Instead the happiness of everybody being a brother, a sister, a friend,
you wouldn't be alone drowning,
nobody would let you sink;
they'd be there to help you swim.

If only people would look for the beauty within,
every person would be family and kin,
that's how God wanted it from the beginning to the end.
Look to their soul, not what's on the outside,
for a person's heart and soul is what makes them,
not the clothes or appearance or the car that they drive.

The beauty within,
search for it my friend,
I have, and yes, seen a lot of darkness and sin,
so many hearts and souls have been broken and beaten down again and again.
So help them along the way,
a simple smile can make their day,
help them with what you say.

You can make a difference of seeing someone laying on the ground and picking them up and showing them the difference of standing tall and placing them where they really belong.

Look for the beauty within,
don't cripple but make a friend,
faith, hope and love are so important in life and the greatest of these is love.

Dana S. Redman

THE BOX

Here you sit on my table,
seem so distant and unable.
Being so full of life and strong,
when I lost you my life went wrong.
It wasn't meant to be,
I pictured us fishing and hunting until we were unable or couldn't see.
Trapping and gathering in the woods,
teaching our grandchildren like we would,
but here you sit in a box,
no more trapping the mink and fox.

What's left of you is no longer strong only your memory lives on and on.
It will never die, for I will never say goodbye.
Every day I ache for you my brother, my friend, my other, too.
I cry inside everyday
spread those ashes where you want to stay,
wishing you would of never went away.
Miss the stories and the tales of your life down there in that hot, ass hell.
Oh I know you miss this place, tired of that fast rat race,
looking forward to retirement,
now all you left is your ashes in this environment.
I will put you where you longed,
that peaceful place you loved all along.
Down in the swamp will be that space.
The final destination, your dream escape.

Where peace and tranquil walk hand in hand.
I'll leave you there,
but never forgotten my dear,
dear friend.

Dana S Redman

The Crane Bird Clan

She's had a hard life, through turmoil and sacrifice.
Trying to forget the pain, the invisible tears that have fell like rain.
She's from the crane bird clan, a beautiful woman, who's wore her brand. Hard to trust any man, she's honest and loyal and too my hand. I wonder, if I'm good enough to stand beside her where she stands. Her escape is to walk away as fast as she can.
No pain felt, no hurt dealt,
no more scares on her heart or welts.

She touches me and my heart melts,
she's strong on the outside and smiles as she hurts,
she doesn't even acknowledge or see her self-worth.
A troubled childhood, a broken home, left its scars and festered thorns.
She's buried deep,
down inside behind the walls that she hides.

She's curled up there in a ball,
crying uncontrollably behind her thick walls.
On the outside she's smiling, too proud to show she's crying.
Too strong to give in, but too scared to love from within.
The crane bird clan,
must be a strong tribal band.

God, how I love her, if she just lets me in,
and then there is me so broken from the past and hurtful misery.
She sees past all the pain and fear,
she knows my heart; she's dried my tears.

Her voice is so soothing to my ears and my soul,
I went to crawl into her, a solid place I can go.
If she would someday just let me in,
I would lay by her side and comfort her until the tears have dried.
Hug her and hold her until the pain will subside.

In that moment I pray to the Lord,
if I can just heal her then maybe I will heal too.
Just by the love of God and a member of the Crane Bird Clan too.

Dana S. Redman

THE HEX

Insects flying, day is dying,
it's too late to be fly tying.
The bugs are hatching,
it's time for catching.
Flip it up above that hole,
let it drift and soon you'll know,
hear the slurp, feel the jerk,
this beats the hell out of work.

Line a zinging, reel a singing, water flying from the run.
Horse him out or you'll have none.
Land him on the sandbar quick,
before he gets off and give you the slip.

Bats a flying, coyotes crying, deer snorting as you wade by whippoorwills singing in the field.
Fireflies dancing on the banks, reminders of all that Mother Nature yields.

Feel the rise, always a surprise
and then the weight, it's no little eight.
Then comes the fight as the pole bends,
he'll fight hard right until the end,
the cline killer has done it again.

As I look over at the bank I can almost see the faces of the great fly fisherman of the past,
Happy Father's Day Dad.
I love you thanks for passing on one of many things you've share and taught me that will last.

Dana S. Redman

The Mist

I see them in the mist, the ones I love the ones I miss.
I see the mist in the evening lair, I see their faces and feel despair.
All I lost is out there.
They're in the mist I can shake my arms in anger and pump my fist, they're in the mist.
So man, loved ones made the list, the passing away, the loss on a list.
They're out there but near in the mist, no more hugs, no more kiss.
I see their faces, feel the ache of the miss,
I reach for them to touch, but it's just a wish.

I miss them so and want them back, the emptiness of their lack.
I see their faces everywhere, I miss their love and their care.
I must go on and live for them, but the emptiness makes just despair.
More than I can bare.

They're out there in mist, they made heavens list.
Now they're blessed by God's hands and kiss.
I'm stuck here in the bliss, trudging on each day closer to the list.
Someday hoping to make that list, be reunited is my wish.

Dana S. Redman

WALKED AWAY

She said she would walk away,
I wasn't good enough for her to stay.
my own insecurities pushed her away.
I think of her and miss her each and all day.
A Christian girl that loved me too,
but I let her walk like we were through.
Not ready for a relationship,
too scared to fail her and enjoy her encouragement.
So much she is to my heart and soul,
so much I looked forward to be with her and grow old.
I lost my hold,
she walked away,
I cry each night and then I pray.
Hope someday she'll still be free,
so I can love her and she love me.

She walked away and I can't blame her,
she's so wonderful that I questioned what she sees.
Now I question me, for she is free,
she lost hope and let me be.

I fell in love, but like a falconry
I cut the leather and cast her to the sky.
Now my heart aches and my soul had died.
She will forget that I exist,
oh how I'll miss her loving hugs and her tender kiss.

She's gone for good into the abyss,
she will find a better man at my loss and my change and miss.
I love her laugh and the way she makes me feel.
When she looks into my eyes I feel so surreal,
she's the real deal.
She loved me true and honest,
she took my heart and made me heal,
but I got scared of what I feel.
She walked away and I see her go,
wish she knew how I love her so.

Dana S. Redman

WAS THE GRASS GREENER

Was the grass greener on the other side,
then where you stood with your love and pride.
Was it greener looking where you once stood,
is it better or for the better good.
Was the decision clear and fair,
how heartache you caused, how much despair.
Was it justifiable,
do you feel the same and as reliable?

Was the grass greener in the pasture on the other side of that fence,
or do you feel empty and can't find the evidence.
So many you hurt for the one,
all the heartaches and commitments undone.
Is it greener where you stood,
do you wish you could go back if you could? Jumping fences is a dangerous game,
so many heartaches, so much pain.
So many disappointments so much guilt and self-blame.

Will your life ever be the same?
Will God forgive you for the shame,
how long do you walk with a heart that's maimed?
There's no jealousy like Abel and Cain,
just an emptiness in your heart and plenty of tear stains.
Loneliness is your constant companion guilt is your name,
and heartache is left in the grass for the trespassing and the shame.

Dana S. Redman

Wet a Line

Sitting in a boat in a lake fishing with a friend,
how great to be fishing again.
Sun on my back,
butt in a boat,
wetting a line and telling jokes.
Oaring around on lake like glass,
reminiscing about fishing in the past.

Fishing with my dad when I was kid,
loved every time that we did.
Whether on a creek, river or lake,
every time was just great.

Wet a line,
where ever you fish, it's a good day to unwind.
Fishing with your kids, fishing with friends,
fishing with your lover, your fishing again.

Wet a line,
you don't catch anything it's still all fine,
need this time.
Memories made, fish filleted, loons swimming, eagles flying overhead,
fish till it's time to go to bed.

Wet a line,
take the time,
make the memories that last forever,

family, friends, being together,
taking fish off of kids hooks, untangling lines,
hooking bait, make memories that are fine,
any day fishing is great.

Just wet a line,
look into your lover's eyes know their heart, read their mind,
enjoy the time.

So when you're tired of the same old rut,
go back in the leaf pile and dig up some worms and stuff.
Grab your wife, kids and friends,
Wet a line every chance you can,
before you don't get a chance when some one's life ends.

Wet a line every time so you don't have to think,
one of these days should have done more,
before it's too late.

Dana S Redman

What Makes a Man

What makes a man,
is it what he can give or what he can take,
how he lives or how he forsakes.
How hard he works to provide,
how honest he is or that he never lied.
How he sweat to exist.

What makes a man,
everything he's worked to have,
how there's days it's hard to smile because life is that sad.

What makes a man,
besides the obvious of God's blood and hands,
a parent's love and plan.

What makes a man,
how tall he stands, or what he stands for.
The money he makes or great integrity and being dirt poor.

What makes a man,
the miles he's walked in hot sand
or working in bitter cold days with frigid hands.
Years of work and toil, has left its mark, calluses and scars are his proof.

What makes a man,
the color of his skin or deeper within,
is he judged on what he has or doesn't in materialistic possessions,
or is he judged on his heart, giving and caring.

What makes a man,
the arthritis in his joints, worn and torn down body from years of labor
or sacrifice to take care of his own.
People are so quick to judge and slow to love,
and what is good is never enough.
Accumulation of memories is the key
and passing on your love and knowledge to your seed.

So what makes a man,
it's not what he has or does not have,
it's his heart and soul,
a place that so many don't take the time to go or know.
Every soul is God's temple which makes each and every one of us essential.

Dana S. Redman

What's Important

Don't matter who I know or how far I've been.
what matters in where I'm going and who I am.
What matters is the love of family and friends that touched me so,
everything else in live can come and go.
The most solid things in life will always stand in God, family, and friends.
The road may be rough,
but don't feel you're alone and have to be that tough.

When you feel down smile and get rid of that frown,
for where ever you're going where ever your bound.
You have friends and family to help you from falling to the ground.
Even an oak drops its acorns as solid as it can be,
but it still shades them and stands over them all.
To protect and nurture them even in the fall.
It's not so much in the destination of your trip but in the travel in all you did.

Dana S. Redman

WHERE'S THE EVE IN ADAM

Where's the Eve in Adam,
why couldn't she love him when she had him?
Why couldn't trust just come naturally, why so much misery,
like picking fruit from a forbidden tree.

Where's the Eve in Adam,
why did the love bring hurt and a heart sadden?
Where's the solace, the safety net,
where's the all give and not much to get.
The sharing, caring and respect.

Where's the Eve in Adam,
why couldn't she love him when she had him?
Why the simple words just stab him?
Words cut and hurt deeper than any physical blow.
Bruises heal and go away but hurtful words are buried deep and stay.
Unfortunately, to never go away.
You hurt, you ache, you cry, you pray.
Hoping for the healing and that it comes soon someday.

Love conquers all, as long as you can tear down the walls,
life can really make you feel small.
Where's the Eve in Adam, why couldn't she show him love when she had him,
the temptation of sin or just not letting him in, is the inevitable ending of them.
The damage of the past,

can hurt the future and a love will last,
but the heartache and pain left, a permanent scare and stain.
You must love the other even more,
for in a relationship no one can keep score.

Trust, love, and forgiveness is the solid foundation for love to be let in us.
Faith, love and hope will follow suit,
unless the pain of the past is to strong and rebuke.

Dana S. Redman

WHERE'S TOMORROW

If tomorrow never comes and you never have a chance to say goodbye.
Only have the question of the unfair why.
The tears run down your face and you can't help but cry.
Your heart is heavy and the unexpected loss of a loved one that dies.
Where's tomorrow in the sadness,
one tragic incident can take away your gladness.
Life is shattered, so precious its true,
never again a chance to say I love you.

A family member gone for good,
but you can't bring them back.
If you could, you would.

Dana S Redman

Will I Measure

Will I measure, will I fit in,
will I pass through your walls to live within?
Will I live inside your soul,
or will I fail and you'll tell me to go.
Will I succeed or will I fail,
will my ship make the storm or sink for my vessel couldn't sail?
Will I fail to stay on the track and be derailed if I lack.
Will I fail inside your arms wide open,
will I chase your doubt and uncertain?
Will my heart take your pain,
will my love erase the stains?
Will my smile chase your tears from your past empty years?
You found me at my worst.
Will you hold my cup for you I thirst?
Will I be your heart and soul to stay,
for your etched in mine the rest of my days.
When my last breath leaves my chest,
your name and your love will be my last gasp.

Dana S. Redman

Worthless

You were the worth; I am the less.
You were the positive and I was the mess.
I was the worse, you were the best.
Now my meaning is worth less.
I never could accept I was great to you,
let too much manipulation tear me through, so I'm worthless.

You've moved on and let me go,
for I wasn't enough to me for you,
so I hurt you and tore your heart and trust in two.
If only I believed that I was great,
and you showed me that I was worth the time in your life, to conversate.

Now I'm here, wish you were near,
but let failure intervene as I contemplate.
I broke everything that I was to you,
broke the trust that we knew.
I now am what I deserve a worthless person that won't be heard.
So said you are a strong woman, you're this and that,
to me that's a line of crap.

Your busy burying your pain in work and staying busy to avoid the hurt.
You never seemed to have time for me,
you say I was in your heart and always on your mind.
You never seeked me out, I was always the go to guy, but wasn't worth the time and find.
Too worthless for you to pine.
So walk away and leave me behind for I'm no good for your kind.

I'm worth less, your worth more,
I'll pick up the pieces that fell to the floor,
for I'll never be trusted by you Ms. Knorr.

I broke your heart, trust and integrity.
So you go out to a bar to be noticed like a celebrity.
You give your number to a man,
I deserve it, but don't understand.
If you really loved me too,
then you would have made a little more time for me and you.
Maybe meet me half way one day, instead of expecting me to be the one to go to you each time,
sorry is all I can say and you are on my mind.
You hear it every day I'm fixing me,
I am apparently not good enough to take the time for, so I'll let you be.
I'll sit here and pine in my cedar home
just an empty shell when you're here all alone.

It's nothing to me like I am to you.
Worthless every day since I lied and hurt you.

I'll never earn your trust or gain it back.
I am a worth less to you for being weak and short on the lack.
I truly love what you are to me, questioned what I was to you when I was always the go to guy,
but you didn't want to be the go to girl at least not for me.
So you'll do better and you will go out,
for all I did is give you doubt and ripped what love you had in your heart out.
I am so sorry that I am me, I wanted to be yours truly.

I don't want to be where I am,
but not the time or the wait because you need a man.
I hope you take the time for him,
so when he's drowning, help him swim.

Go to him and make yourself included,
or eventually his heart and mind will be polluted,
with doubt and fear and failure too.
One thing for sure we both did wrongs, even though the love is true.
Go be with a man and tell me if it makes you feel better,
or will it just take another piece of you away that kept you together.

Smile your smile as you cry inside I know I done wrong, I know I lied,
but can you be with another with what you really feel inside.
I can't and won't even though you tell me too.
I want my memory to be you,
so how can I be that low,
when my heart is yours and you keep it in your soul.
Go see other guys, for that's what you want,
I hope every time you do; you see me right there too.
A constant reminder that worth less or not that we truly love each other,
but failure and doubt broke each other's wall too.
Until then remember I love you.

Dana S. Redman

Wounded Bird

You went so long like a wounded bird,
going unseen and unheard.
You've struggled so long to survive,
but no one seen or heard your cry,
to take the time to look and ask why,
and all you wanted to do is fly.

So you hid during the day and hid in the dark,
but I took the time to look, my lark.
You're wounded, but so worth mending,
I want to throw you up and watch you fly in the sending.
Coast on the breeze and fly with ease,
Soar high but don't ever leave me.
Even when you're not around and I find myself feeling down,
I come around, in you I see.

So I'm going to search high and low,
look in the brush and grasses slow,
helping you is all I know.
My biggest fear is letting you go.

Wounded bird,
you're being picked up and will be healed by me.
I will hold you in my hands until you want to be free,
I'll watch you fly as far as I can see.
Hopefully you'll come back and someday find me.

Dana S. Redman

You Are

What you are is my partner at work,
the one who can get away with calling me a jerk.
The one who cares for me more than anyone,
The one who nurtures me when I'm broken or hurt.
You're my vision that I see every day,
you're the foot on the pedal when I'm in a hurry to see you and listen to what you have to say.
You're morning coffee like only you make,
you're the drunken pork chops that are to die for when you can cook them that way.
You're the fire in me when I feel so cold,
You're the comfort of life that I won't be along when I'm old.
You're the reason that God sent you my way and same just for you,
a reason for the day.

You're my confidence, my partner for all time.
You're the buzz I get that's better than wine.
You're my beautiful when the day seems so gray.
You are the reason the sun comes out after the rain tried to stay.
You're my partner out in the woods
or out on a lake or shopping for goods.
You're the annoying creatures that drive me so mad.
God has blessed us both, and I sure am so glad.
I love you more than you know,
You're my season, rain, sun and snow.
No matter the weather as long as you're close,
the sun will be shining where you are the most.
I love you.

Dana S. Redman

You'll Find Another

You'll find another,
find one when you'll be discovered.
Not in a bar or in a dark place,
someone to love you when they see your bright face.
Someone who sees all I saw,
someone to love you for who you are.

You'll find another around your age,
forget all about me and turn the page.
You'll find someone to take care of you,
love you no matter what you say or do.

You'll find another to be your man and be true.
Throw me away and find a new,
someone to pick you up and not make you blue.
Love you for they're a woman and a mother,
just give it time and you'll be discovered.
You'll find another that don't mind being smothered.
Someone who is understanding, not selfish or demanding.
Catch you no matter where you're landing,
and be right there where you're standing.
You'll find another and love you like no other.
You'll find another better than me,
Just give it time and you will see.
You'll find another...

Dana S. Redman

Footnote

Relationships are like buying shoes, when they're new, they feel good and comfortable, but after time they break down. If they're not well built with love and care and don't have a great soul they'll break down and fall apart and won't be a great pair.

A "footful" thought by Dana S. Redman

I know dogs go to heaven, because they're the only creature on earth that loves unconditionally like God himself.

Dana S. Redman

Paper & Pen

I wish I was paper 'n pen, then you would love me until the end. I threw the words away, the trust, hope, faith, anything I say. Like a piece of paper in the rain, I will deteriorate into the ground. Lost into the ecosystem to never be found, for I let real love down. I wish I was paper and pen, to read over and over, and over again, but short comings broke what that once strong, and a beautiful woman was hurt from my wrong. None expecting that I myself was worth enough all along.

Dana S Redman

GETTING BY

I find the sun to chase the rain, find the good among the pain. Write the feelings on paper that are tear stained. Question the loss as I still remain, why so many are gone but in my heart and brain they remain, so many good ones pass before their time, but Gods plan is one that is not in vain.

Love conquers all, but with love comes pain or valid enough in her heart to belong. So I erased what was written on her heart with my scribe, destroyed so much with my actions and lie and now her and I both despise me. I ripped out the pages of our chapter too soon. I still lover her so, but doubt was my doom.

Dana S Redman

DEDICATION

I dedicate this book to my three best friends:

Gustav S. Redman,
Not only were you my father, but you were my scholar, my teacher, my hero, and best friend.

Jon F. Schondelmayer,
You are and always will be a brother to me. We taught, shared, and enjoyed so many adventures, dreams, laughter and tears, but like my dad, a lifetime of memories I hold close to my heart.

Robert (Bobby) J. Wilk,
We taught each other and learned together and made so many memories that were always great times.

These fine men left me here to live for them, for we all would die for each other. I love you all and miss you dearly, thank you for your love and without rarely saying it, you always showed it.

Love,
Dana

Printed in the United States
By Bookmasters